Tell The Truth, Shame The Devil

By. Dr. Rasul EL

Allah's Truth Circle
ATC Publishing

Artwork by: Seanre Benette

Illustration by: Keenan Ewin-Walk

Edited by: Malaika. A

ISBN 978-0-9939768-0-3

briskinthehouse@gmail.com

Twitter: @BriskInTheHouse

Dedication

This book is dedicated to all Original people dispersed throughout the wilderness of North America. May this book aid in your healing and help break the chains of mental slavery put on us through the global system of White supremacy.

Table of Contents

Forward

We are living in a time where what's hidden will be broadcasted and the half-truths that have been broadcasted will be chastised. This is the main reason why I've decided to edit this book.

As a fellow author, I, like Rasul, feel the need to produce publications that will edify the minds of our readers. This book will shed light on much of the misinformation that has been disseminated from the 'powers that be.'

"Are we born unknowing or are we born knowing all?" This question is the foundation of the content of this publication. In fact, you will come across material in this book that will make you think it's a complete falsification. Should you feel the need to question the authenticity of anything you read in this particular publication, feel free to do the research for yourself.

There is a difference between information and knowing what to do with the information after you have received it. They say, "Ignorance is bliss." This statement can lead to the mentality that what you don't know will not hurt you. Unfortunately, what you don't know can be the very thing that leads to your ultimate demise.

Tell the Truth, Shame the Devil will be one of those publications that will make you thankful you came across the material you are about to come across. Why? Because it will heighten your sense of awareness in this dimension. With that sense of awareness comes accountability. Therefore, you are responsible for what you do once you learn something new.

Without further ado, enjoy the shift and expansion of your perspective while reading *Tell the Truth, Shame the Devil.*

Sincerely,

Felicia El-Bey

Introduction

We are all programmed in one way or another. Anyone who thinks otherwise is the most programmed.

Anything can be programmed. It is natural to condition the body for optimum potential. However, half the things we are programmed to do are being used against us, without our consent. How is this possible? The CIA has manuals on how to correctly manufacture a response. It's called, "Brainwashing".

The CIA has been using this technique since the 1930's. Most Original people know they are oppressed but can't unify to fight the oppressor. We have documented history of slavery, lynchings, and the strategically implemented presence of drugs and guns in the so-called Black communities to reinforce White supremacy. We participate in this society out of fear or programming.

We have proof that the powers that be have never changed their behavior. Their madness has been going on for 6000 years. I believe they shouldn't be allotted another minute.

Media has always been used to convey a message to the community. Oral tradition was our way of life until writing was used to keep records of the past. We told stories of magnificent deities that broke science and order of law and used symbols that spoke to parts of our brain now dormant in this society.

Prophet Noble Drew Ali said, "If you do not occupy your mind it is because someone or something else has". The things we do on impulse are influenced by our environment. For example, we have all been to the mall and seen posters for sales on the window and left with a couple bags in our hands. This society is the most manipulated in world history.

The first law of nature is self-preservation. Naturally, you would never make choices that would affect you negatively (especially when trial and error is the foundation of what most call, "common sense"). If you informed most people that they're eating poison, they will reply, "I know but it tastes so good". Responses like that are evidence of indulging in the lower self. Prophet Noble Drew Ali also said, "If you seek the devil, look no further than yourself". Devil is being used in this context to refer to your lower self. So what is keeping the devil active in you?

We are influenced by our surroundings. Most of us wouldn't know who Jesus Christ was if slavery wasn't introduced to us. The letter J was not invented until the 16th century. It's only 400-500 years old. This means the name Jesus is something people agreed upon and isn't based on fact. Most historical accounts are based on lies. We know nothing about ancient times, just American history. We have tribes in the America's that can trace their history back as far as 50,000 years. They didn't call themselves Indians or Africans. Most cultures believe in, "honor thy mother and thy father so thy days will be longer on this land". The thing about history is it has a way of connecting you with a way of life that has been tried and tested. You must have lived over 26,000 years in order to make a calendar that is 26,000 years. You must be a great and knowledgeable people to have been here for over 26,000 years. In those times, living civilized, in peace and in harmony with nature and the Creator was second nature.

The "White man" has only been here 6000 years. He will not be here 100 years from now (Inshallah). 2000 years of their history was spent living in caves, not being able to walk up right. They didn't bathe and only started bathing 700 years ago. They used to eat each other and always lived in a hostile environment. Even in present times, America is only 238 years old, has had 6 world wars, and has had countless civil wars (including the war on drugs).

The United States of America has never known a time of peace and no human being can function correctly in their stressful society. There are civilizations that have known peace for thousands of years and produced fine arts and sciences because of it. You can't build pyramids without having peace. War was not on the mind of Egyptians as they built pyramids. They never owned prisons and obviously didn't have criminals (which might sound surprising to someone who lacks knowledge of self). This society has provided the world with cigarettes and hamburgers. Even the things that do come in handy radiate us with extra low frequencies (ELF).

We pay more for the food they *don't* poison. The powers that be are so evil they charge you extra *not* to genetically modify the food. Why would we abandon the ways of our forefathers and mothers for the ways of this civilization?

Chapter 1: The Disconnect

I was watching an interesting documentary on the brain one night called, "The Secret Life of the Brain." It was about a man that suffered a severe stroke which ended up paralyzing half of his body. The strange part about how the stroke affected him was it killed hundreds of millions of brain cells. This has affected his emotional awareness. He also has trouble making everyday decisions because he lost the emotional connection to his past. Memory and emotions guide every decision we make.

Now, back in slavery, we were punished for doing anything that resembled what our ancestors and forefathers did to make us great. The punishment for being Melinated has been going on for too long for us to not notice it. So, when we identify with anything original or African, we see it as primitive or inferior to what this civilization has provided the world (which in reality has been nothing but slow death).

People seem to forget that the Europeans that were sent to the Americas to colonize it were criminals and misfits freely released out of prisons. This society since, its inception, was built on criminal activity. They also happen to be the biggest drug pushers in the world. For you to identify with this society means you agree with a certain degree of criminality that comes with it. It's a "Dog-Eat-Dog" world on this side of the map. We don't help uplift fallen humanity because we are too busy surviving. It's the stress and fear that is used to control our emotions and behavior.

This society is based off of a reward-punishment system that was created by B.F Skinner. You are rewarded when you do things to further this society, mostly with money and privilege. Most go to school to obtain a government job or some sort of job that assists in keeping this society running smoothly. It could be a police officer, lawyer, president, accountant, social worker, and so on and so forth. These jobs are made for keeping the social order. A police man is the policy keeper who makes sure you follow the rules and regulations of policies put together by politicians who are paid by us to do so. The definition of policy is a principle or protocol to guide decisions. The question is why are we getting our principles from people who obtained this land by taking it from you? These people are not governed by Love, Truth, Peace, Freedom, Justice, and/or Equality. They have never known peace. Even the sun torments them. If their principle was what is best for us, wouldn't we freely choose to follow it? Why do they need to force us to follow their principles? Why do they think we can't make decisions for ourselves?

We have been a free thinking, advanced set of people for millions of years so why would we need someone to make our decisions for us (unless there is an outcome they are trying to manufacture and control the response of the people for their benefit)?

People of color are practicing socialization in this society. Socialization is the process of people acquiring knowledge, social skills, and language to be able to conform to the workings of a society. I am 100% confident it is not your knowledge of self or your Kemetic/Nubian/African original language that made you qualify for the job you went to school for. If anything, that will be the reason why you don't get hired, because having knowledge of self means they can't control you and you might not take orders very well. Most doctors from foreign countries, like India, can't find jobs when they come over here because they weren't trained in this country. Pretty much they are saying you must be indoctrinated to receive the doctorate which is the academic degree needed in order to work in certain fields such as health care. Now, if the human body is the same all around the world, wouldn't that person qualify to treat the human body no matter what side of the planet he is on?

I plan on going to school for Holistic Health Sciences and I know once I finish, I won't be obtaining employment at the Doctor's Office. Doctors aren't trained to heal; they are trained to prescribe pills and let you know the date of surgery and are compensated handsomely for doing so.

Socialization has made us abandon who we are. How many times have you been on a job and had to talk a little bit "Whiter" just so you don't make other people feel uncomfortable? Socialization makes you conform to the environment you're in but the things you lose in the process can make you hostile towards others on your down time.

This is the stress we live under as a people on a daily basis. We fear not being accepted by this society so we do things to blend in. Every organization that ever came to the aid of Original people was infiltrated by the FBI and had its members compromised one way or another. In fact, the FBI was formed to keep the Original man of North America down in the wilderness of North America. It was created to stop the rise of the

Black Messiah. Most of the leaders for those so-called Black organizations were punished with death or imprisonment.

For example, to train rats to run mazes and stand on its own legs on command, you shock it when it doesn't do what you want. On the other hand, you feed it when it does what you want. After a while, you won't have to command the rat to do anything because it will do what you want it do so it doesn't get shocked again.

Just like the example given with the rats, you see this in our people now who accept their conditions and feel they can't do anything about it. Our memory is so short we forget when Dr. Martin Luther King Jr. crippled a town by boycotting bus services for a year. They had bus drivers getting laid off left and right until they had to make a deal with the people to bring the boycott to an end.

We forget there was a time when the Negro Baseball League was more exciting and making more money than the major league baseball games. The only reason they brought Jackie Robinson in and broke the color barrier was to get the so-called Black consumer dollars. We are only useful to these people when we can make money for them and they reward you with the little crumbs that fall from the table.

There was a time when we had a Black Wall Street in Oklahoma, which was a thriving city with thousands of so-called black millionaires making more money than the so-called "Whites." They developed group economics amongst themselves. They say the money passed through 10 times before it went outside the community. If you are familiar with this history, then you know the end result of those Original peoples' success. The white man burned that shit to the ground and not one person survived and no one went to jail for this crime.

It turned out the people that burned it down worked in the police force, some were judges and lawyers, social workers, and plain ol' KKKackers. Til' this day, with all the wars the United States of America has ever been in, Black Wall Street was the only time America was ever bombed by air. They dropped napalms on the city, bombed it from the sky and the ground, just to make sure they got everything and everyone. Most Original people did not know this history until a so called White president, named Bill Clinton, brought it to our attention.

These people have us under such mind control that we don't realize the wrong they do to us (unless they point it out). If it doesn't show up on the 6 o'clock news, it generally does not exist.

For instance, we had an epidemic of propaganda when one man named Joseph Kony was supposedly terrorizing parts of Uganda. It turned out to be a hoax put together by the United States Media department. People that actually lived in the country had no idea these rumors were being spread. As a matter of fact, most people found out it was a false alarm when they called their family members out of panic to find out if everything was alright.

This is almost the case with every, "War Rebel" story found in American news. They use the propaganda and hysteria generated by the people as an excuse to invade in the name of help and AID (such as The Red Cross). Once western civilization enters a foreign country, it never leaves and they force their ways onto the people of that nation. People are never the same after the introduction of western civilization and are always affected negatively.

As we speak, Israel is bombing Palestine, killing innocent people and the U.S government condones and funds all these actions. Western civilization funds the Jews because they are the same people. Another name for this is called Zionism (which we will expound on in future volumes for this series).

Now, as a person with morals, how could you say you support anything that has to do with western civilization? The funny thing is most people that bring this knowledge to the awareness of the masses get punished for doing so. The most famous tactic by this society to silence someone is character assassination. Most politicians are blackmailed into keeping the agenda of white supremacy afloat in this society. They will say the individual molested children or bring up dirt from their past to embarrass them into seclusion or apparent suicide. How many entertainers in the past 40 years have died from suicide or drug over dose? Only people uneducated on universal laws will leave it up to coincidence.

The government and media play off of our fear and fascination with mystery. We believe too much. The definition of belief is something one accepts as true or real; a firmly held opinion. Everything about this society is based on theory. They have a theory for everything. Big Bang Theory, Theory of Relativity, Theory of Evolution, Film Theory, Chaos Theory, and so on. There is nothing concrete with these people.

The first thing you should know is a theory is as good as the paper it was written down on, meaning it means nothing until proven right or wrong through observation and experimentation. They have a Theory of Evolution because they would rather come from apes and sea organisms than to say they came from the Original man. Living off theory means you're not living off facts and truth. The closest you will get living off of theory is generalizations and stereotypes (which has affected us greatly).

Everyone's foundation should be knowledge and information. Knowledge and information are used for everyday decision making. Without it, we wouldn't be able to make the most beneficial choices in life. Actions and deeds normally reflect how well one applies information once it's learned. When you have information that benefits your life and don't apply it, you should really ask yourself, "Why?".

Again, this falls down to programming. For instance, most smokers are desensitized to the images of black lungs and hearts that come on the package of cigarettes. Sometimes, you have to ask yourself, "Are my thoughts really my own?". Also, how many times have you sung a song you hated after you were forced to listen to it in your car? When you hear or see something repetitively, eventually it gets locked into the subconscious part of your brain. Most of the time, we are too distracted by another sense to even notice this occurring.

Now, apply this repetition in everyday life and you can see how your environment can shape you. When you turn on the television, you are bombarded by images attacking your subconscious mind. Music videos, shows, and news broadcasts (just to name a few). It is 2015 and we still can't get an accurate portrait of biblical times. They just released a movie called, "Noah" with Russell Crowe starring as Noah. To the date, with all the books, information, YouTube videos, and lectures, they still portray Jesus and Noah as white. With that said, it's obvious they are not doing this because of a lack of knowledge. They are doing it to attack the minds of Melinated people. They use these movies and TV shows to project an alternate reality where melanin generally doesn't exist. They must show themselves in the dominant position at all times. They know that positive imagery shapes the functions of the brain. There is no difference between reality and pretension because once you start seeing images of original people portrayed as civilized and great, you might start believing you're great (which is half way to knowing you are great).

Something inside of you will become aware of itself and start guiding you to think for your Self. See, self-hatred is necessary for this society. It is a political necessity to have Original people out of their mind. If a people have no culture, they can be given one and made servants to white supremacy. When you have an identity and culture, it gives you rules and guide lines to things you will and won't do. It gives you a code of conduct and a sense of pride you are willing to defend. When you identify with your ancestors as being physical Gods on Earth, you start trying to achieve things they achieved, you start walking in the will of God.

Most Greek gods are really stories made from the life of people in Africa. Imhotep is a perfect example.

The Greeks called him, "Asklepios". If you watch, "The Mummy" you will see the father of medicine demonized as the evil foe they must defeat to save the world.

Apply this to real life now on subjects like the "War on Terror". We know Bin Laden was a CIA agent trained and funded by the United States government. We know 9/11 was a hoax and another attack on the United States by the United States. The U.S will take a good guy and paint him as the bad guy in order to gain supporters, and vice versa. They did this with Saddam Hussain, Fidel Castro, and Gaddafi (just to name a few). To this day, it's hard to speak about the honorable Elijah Muhammad without people associating him with the murder of Malcolm X or having children with multiple women who he seduced (both are false accusations but you know how propaganda works).

Now, the question is: how do we fall for this trick every time around? When people are unsure what to believe, I always say go with the opposite of what you heard. If they advise you to take flu shots, you better avoid them at all cost.

The biggest problem we have is we trust the source of information. We truly believe this government has our best interest at heart. The thought of how this government came into power never seems to cross peoples minds. If you talk to the average person, they think things have always been like this. Movies alone will have you thinking an ancient White man actually existed. The so called, "White" man has never had a dynasty and a prophet has never been sent to them to redeem them. Judging by the news feed, it seems even nature is trying to get rid of them. Trusting a source of information can be dangerous because sometimes you forget to question things out of confidence.

Most of us cannot receive information if it wasn't qualified by the European. Part of the reason why we can't unite as a people is because some of us trust our oppressor to the point of worshipping. We are scared to investigate the unknown and this fear is showing up in our people through disease.

Kidney disease is on the rise in so-called Black people; we suffer from kidney disease more than any other race in the wilderness of North America. That is because fear is stored in our kidney and it is causing our organs to shut down. No one can operate efficiently under constant stress.

Stress is the number one killer of people in general. There is nowhere on the planet we are not under stress.

When I speak of western civilization, I'm not just talking about the wilderness of North America. Western civilization has invaded the world with its companion of white supremacy used as a global system of control. This has caused famines in some countries and genocide in others. The U.S funds both parties and watches them go to war safely from the view of a television screen. The rabbit hole goes deep but that is no excuse not to face what is right in front of you.

I haven't even got into how Katrina affected us as a people because if one thing was for sure, we were left to fend for ourselves. To this day, those people haven't moved back to their homes, and when the government gave them a trailer to stay in, it was filled with asbestos.

We have never been given a fair shot living in western civilization. It literally is not designed for us. Abiding by the rules of this society will only destroy us.

Chapter 2: Maniac European Devils In Action (MEDIA)

For this next chapter, I want to concentrate on media and how powerful it can be when used by a friend or foe.

The media has always been used to convey a message to the masses since the beginning of time. Oral tradition and stories passed down from father to son is a rite of passage, where many tribes and nations get their culture from. In Jesus' (Isa) time media was used to announce that the Son of God has arrived in certain cities and town (whether they were happy about it or not).

Media is used to spread the news to keep the people in the community aware of what is going on around them.

Humans have made migrations all over the earth for millions of years. Some continents that Original people migrated from like Atlantis and Lemuria are not even in existence anymore. How did these people know to all migrate and move together in the 1000's to populate other pieces of land?

A perfect example of this is the ancient Kushites who migrated and moved to the Indus Valley. Once they inhabited that area, it was known as Indus Kush (which we now know today as India). How did the people get the news to move as a unit to another piece of land and start another great civilization that mirrored their own? We use to sit around camp fires staring at the flickering flames, being entranced while a griot or elder told stories of times of old and mythological stories that open parts of the mind subconsciously without the conscious mind knowing.

See in ancient times, our ancestors knew that the most important part of the mind is the subconscious mind. Once something enters the subconscious mind, it is programmed into you; this is where our personalities and habits reside. The God part of you dwells in this part of the mind. The subconscious mind is so powerful that your life is actually a result of what you or someone else has programmed it with. It gives you what you want whether you know it or not. It is your connection to the universe where the saying, "As Above, So Below" comes from. That's why our ancestors used mantras and meditation to program and condition the mind for great works like building temples and pyramids or living for 100's of years building civilizations that last for 1000's of years. They used deities that represented properties of the self or elements of the universe.

Ptah would be the dark matter of the universe or the melanin inside of you because as previously mentioned, "As Above, So Below". Once you know that controlling your mind is controlling the universe, you will never be a victim again. You will be a master.

This, in essence, is mastery of self (which we all must come to one day in one life time or another). See, when you know your Self, you naturally will program your Self with great things. It's simply called practice.

Me, personally, I programmed my Self with any and everything that has to do with Knowledge of Self. I sleep to lectures and wake up to lectures. I go to my local so-called Black owned store and I consciously make sure every paycheque I get, a certain percentage go towards them. I read every day for a certain amount of hours and make sure I fit my daily meditation into my schedule. This among other things is what I do to reprogram my Self every day because the first thing you learn in psychology is that no one is above being programmed and our subconscious mind is attacked on a daily basis.

There are 2 types of programming. The first is, "General" and the second is, "Specific".

General programming comes from daily operations of living in western civilization from going to school or watching TV. It is all used to manufacture a response in the subject. You are your thoughts and the powers that be know this. If they can control how you think and feel, you will essentially be a slave but with no awareness of it. The Honourable Elijah Muhammad always said times are worse now than slavery because at least then, people knew they were slaves and revolted. We revolted up until the 1960's. What's stopping us from still fighting oppression?

We didn't always just take abuse from our enemies and oppressors. Normally, we band together for a greater cause and created plans to achieve a common goal. This method applies to pyramid building and revolution.

If you were to judge the world from what you seen on the "Tel-Lie-Vision," you would assume something is very wrong with the so-called Black community in the wilderness of North America. We are seen as entertainers never in leading roles that show our true genius. The only time we win an Oscar (whose logo is actually the Kemetic deity Ptah), is when we play degrading roles.

Just, look at Halle Berry and Lupita Nyong'o. I might catch slack for naming Lupita but, come on people, she won because she played a slave. They only see us as slaves. This society is built on a "Master-Slave" relationship.

These movies are used as programming because our subconscious mind does not know the difference between reality and pretension. It's called, "Post Hypnotic Suggestion". They distract one of the many senses, leaving another one wide open to receive what the programmer intends on projecting.

See, people fail to notice, but music can dictate your behavior because it is the only form of energy that can enter your subconscious without your permission. It works by repeating words over and over again. Repetition is the mother of all learning. So, when you hear negative slogans repeated over and over again in today's music, and you never wonder why our youth are acting the way that they do today?

Musicians will always have more favor with young people than any politician will. So, when things like "get money, fuck bitches" is repeated on an ongoing basis, it gets programmed into your subconscious. Now, you can't find a so-called Black man that won't sell out for a little bit of paper.

The only people that worship money is the 10%. Now, 85% of the world worship money due to manipulation by the 10%. However, the 10% didn't need mantras and music to be materialistic. They were born that way. How did this materialism and negativity get into the music? It could be that they infiltrated and used Skinner's Reward/Punishment system. The reward is money and fame and the punishment is silence.

When you watch music videos, sometimes the screen switches too fast for your mind to consciously know what is going on. However, your subconscious mind picks up everything the conscious mind misses. If images were to move slowly across the screen, it would give you time to think about what you are watching. Fast cutting screens in these videos cause a corresponding electrical chemical reaction. It releases endorphins that have a drug like effect on the viewer. They are selling you a lifestyle that was fashioned by the Europeans to drive us out of our Original mind.

Television screens flickering make it worse because the screen is always flickering but you can't see it with your naked eye. If you were to pull out your camera phone and point it at your TV screen, you would see these lines going up and down through the screen. This induces a hypnotic state. The principles of hypnosis are very basic. It's to force your attention of the conscious mind on one or more of the five senses.

In the case of movies and television, they use the sense of sight and sound. The hypnotic state of mind is a natural state of mind we go in and out of during the day. It is a dreamlike state that leaves our subconscious mind open to infiltration. When the conscious mind (which analyzes things before it is internalized) is bypassed, anything can be programmed into you.

Whenever you watch the news, the newscaster is always looking into the camera like he is personally talking to you and he speaks in a sing-song sort of tone. Negro preachers and pastors are experts at applying this technique to grab you. Sing-song patterns of speech always induce trance like states. Just listen to Martin Luther King Jr. or Jesse Jackson speak.

The television plugs into your nervous system and induces a trance like state. No matter what you are watching, you cannot stop it. Look at the effects of television on our children.

Prior to television, ADHD did not exist. The television is like a member of the family. Some people use it to babysit their children when they don't want to give them any attention or may feel they need a break from parenthood.

The only reason children can sit in front of a TV screen and not at school is: firstly, they are in a trance state and secondly, endorphins are being released in the brain, so they are getting a drug like effect and when the child is forced to stop watching the television, you see immediate signs of withdrawal. They become fidgety and can't sit still for more than a minute. They can't sit still because they are looking for the same kind of drug like feeling they get from the television.

The TV disturbs the brain chemistry and induces addictive behavior in people. Most of the time, you don't know you need something until you see it marketed in a commercial. How many times has your child asked you for a toy after they saw the commercial for it while watching cartoons?

Now, the way the TV affects adults is by selling them a fairy tale you agree to without consciously being aware of it.

We have no shows that show us in our prime or at least what we could be. We can't even get a fantasy land where so-called Black people are prospering like Europeans. They cannot give us positive images of ourselves because they know it molds the brain.

Positive images help brain development and of course, boost self-esteem. Societies are built on positive imagery. Just look at the temple walls in Kemet: it always showed the ruling people in a positive light. If movies and TV were just entertainment, why can't they entertain a so-called all Black show where Knowledge of Self and ancient symbolism is incorporated?

At this point, it has nothing to do with money because they own all the money in the world; they even print it when they run out. It's because they know the brain does not know the difference between real and pretension. If you were to see positive images of your history or who you truly are as a Melinated being, you might start equating yourself as being great. A great man can never be a follower. He will question everything and soon find out how much of a falsehood this nation is built on.

In the times of our forefathers, we used art and entertainment as a way to pass down information, morals, knowledge, and anything beneficial for the community. Now? It is used as a vehicle for propaganda for this society's agenda of control and survival.

They have been practicing yellow journalism since the late 1800s. Yellow journalism is a type of journalism that presents little or no legitimate well-researched news and instead, uses eye-catching headlines to sell more newspapers. Techniques may include exaggerations of news events, scandal-mongering or sensationalism. This means even before the TV was invented, they were controlling the news you got. Why else would people be willing to sign up to fight in wars that America funded in the first place?

See, mind control is as basic as controlling information. That's why we say knowledge is power because these people are in positions of power by knowing things you don't. It's really that simple. How else could the minority control the majority (unless the majority is misinformed on who has the power)?

Again, us not fighting back for our rights is a recent thing. In the 1950's, when subliminal programming was brought to the attention of the masses, they found out American industries were researching ways to influence people to buy their products. It caused an uproar and people started protesting, saying it was an invasion of privacy. That invasion of privacy is the mind and they were fighting because no one has the right to be manipulated into doing things they wouldn't normally do (unless they had the right information).

This society openly admits that subliminal programming/messaging is part of its everyday operations and it is not their concern to protect you from it.

There is a very famous experiment where they inserted "Buy Coca-Cola" and "Buy Popcorn" in movie films. The slides in the presentation showed a dramatic increase in sales of the food department. Mind control and propaganda is always trying to sell you something whether it is materialistic or sell you an idea of globalization and white supremacy.

We live in a totally controlled environment and we don't realize the extent of manipulation by unseen forces. Our society is the most controlled and manipulated in history because the programming and conditioning is more advanced. Internet and television make it easy for a propagandist to get their agenda out.

The first object of a propagandist is to create the circumstance that will enlist a state of mind that is optimum for the reception of their message. The perfect example for this is found in the Hegelian Dialectic, which was created by a 19th century German philosopher, Georg Wilhelm Friedrich Hegel. His thesis was based on Problem-Reaction-Solution and how you can manipulate people by these 3 things. They manufacture a problem or take advantage of one already in place in order to get the desired reaction of public outcry whereby, the public demands a solution which has been predetermined from the beginning.

This technique was used on September 11th, 2001, when America was "supposedly" attacked by terrorists and needed to be protected from any further attacks on the nation. However, the U.S. is the real terrorist of America. They bombed their own buildings then invaded another country as a solution for it not to happen again.

You can apply this Problem-Reaction-Solution manipulation to many events in history and see this technique has been in operation for as long as Western civilization has been established. They don't let the left hand know what the right hand is doing.

When these people murder an Original man, they are trying to test how oppressed they have us, they are experimenting on how well they have you controlled. Any solution accepted from society was through manipulation.

Freedom starts in the mind. We must understand the nature of the problem and come up with our own solution. Mind control in the United States of America is a battle of souls. They know the mind is the gateway to the soul and if you don't occupy that space in your mind, it will be open to intruders that will have you acting in ways other than yourself.

It is all about feeding your Self with as much knowledge as possible so you know what to be aware of and how to act accordingly when circumstances occur.

When we talk about the devil taking peoples souls, we are really referring to the pale man replacing our Original mind with his. This causes us to destroy ourselves and making him look innocent in it all. We will blame ourselves before we blame the powers that be. That's how strong this mind control is right now.

The only thing we can blame ourselves for is not rising above this. It is no one else's responsibility to get us out of this mess but ourselves. Until we point out who is friend and who is foe, we will be divided.

For instance, in 1949, a radio station in Ecuador played, "War of The Worlds" as a news broadcast, tricking the people into believing it was the end of world. When the people found out the radio broadcast was a hoax, a big mob formed at the radio station and burned it down. These people joined together and formed a mob for being deceived by a radio station and burned it down. How come we can't join together to protect each other when we know we are hunted by highwaymen (police/bandits) on a daily basis?

Government brutality is at an all-time high right now and it does not look like it is slowing down any time soon. They could not do this to us 50 years ago without us fighting back, but the programming is so sophisticated you don't realize someone has their foot on your neck. When you have a trillion dollars in buying/spending power and have nothing of our own it lets you know the people are being misguided. Someone knows something we don't and they are definitely taking advantage of it.

Tell the Truth, Shame the Devil

Chapter 3: KKKops, Klans, and Highway Men

"The Right hand is never letting you know what the Left hand is doing."

I want to take the time to address all police (highwaymen/bandits) brutality and murders that has occurred this year (2014). It is obvious they are running rituals and experiments on the people to measure where the collective psyche is at the moment. Police murdering Original people is nothing new to this society. These highwaymen who we call police were actually put here to do what they are doing to us right now. The relationship between police has always been a Master-Slave relationship. They were not created to have our best interest at heart.

The police force was started around the reconstruction period of America to police newly free slaves and so-called Blacks. The main participants in forming these highwaymen and bandits were the ADL (Anti-Defamation League) and the KKK (Ku Klux Klan). This was started by Albert Pike who brought Scottish Rite Freemasonry to America. The ADL (one of the most racist groups to ever be created on the face of the earth) started out in South Carolina as Jewish slave holders. They controlled newly reformed Negroes as a law enforcement branch. The ADL fostered the revival of the KKK in post-World War 2.

The reason why no KKK member has ever been tried and charged for lynching a so-called Black person is because they were the law, also known as the police men with white sheets on their off duties. The same people doing the lynching are the same people you are running to for justice and wondering why you never received any. All this terrorism is in place to counteract the reconstruction of building up newly freed slaves and Negroes. This is what you call neo-slavery. They use organizations like the police and FBI (Federal Bureau of Investigation) to control you and keep you from prospering.

We must remember we didn't have prisons and jails in ancient times - Khemit never owned any jail houses and doesn't have the word, "prison" in their language and dialect. Now, that's something to really think about.

We must remember it was the KKK who burned Black Wall Street to the ground and left no survivors. After learning that the KKK, police, and justice department are the same entity, it makes sense why no one went to jail or got charged for air bombing and destroying a whole entire community. The KKK is an advanced secret society and we have no idea because we have the picture of hillbillies and rednecks dressed up in white bed sheets. Most of the members of the KKK were lawyers, judges, police officers, preachers, and other people you would seek refuge in if you needed help in this society. Most of these people are freemasons and if you know anything about Western Freemasonry, you should know the basis of it is to keep the Original man down.

They tell a story of an African God-Man named Hiram Abiff who was summoned to build Solomon's temple. He was an expert at building pillars that support sayings such as, "As above, so below". One day while on his way to work, he was confronted by 3 Ruffians named Jubelo, Jubela, and Jubelum. These Ruffians wanted the secrets to Solomon's tomb and when they didn't get what they wanted, they proceeded to attack Hiram. They gave him 3 blows: one to the chest (heart chakra), second blow to the neck (throat chakra), and a final blow to the head (crown chakra) which killed him. The 3 Ruffians buried his body in a shallow grave.

Freemasons do rituals and take death oaths to keep this African God-Man buried in this shallow grave. This African God-Man represents the so-called Black man in the wilderness of North America. It represents the fact that we are mentally dead because we lost the knowledge of our selves due to slavery. The grave is shallow to show that it is possible to resurrect ourselves when we come into the knowledge of who we are as a people.

Now, apply this mass ritual to what is going on today and you'll make the connection as to why things are going the way they are going. Most police men and government officials are Freemasons. In fact, there are certain government positions you cannot obtain without being a Freemason. These people are all about oaths and secrets. The secret is to keep the original man down by any means necessary. Most slave masters were freemasons during the times of slavery in the Americas. They hated the thought of reconstruction and freeing the Negroes out of slavery. Here is a personal letter a Jewish Freemason wrote to the United States, expressing his feelings on the newly freed Negroes:

"I have always looked with the utmost dread and distrust on the experiment of emancipation so suddenly enforced on the south by the event of the war. God knows how it will all end! The south is kept crushed under Negro rule. I can never consent to go

to New Orleans and break my heart witnessing the rule of Negroes and carpetbaggers. Nothing is as abhorrent to me as Radicalism which seeks to elevate the populace into the governing class."

- Judah P. Benamin

On a side note, the ADL/B'nai B'rith were accused of setting up and orchestrating President Lincoln's assassination. They have so much power and so many connections that everyone on trial for Lincoln's assassination were members of the B'nai B'rith (including Albert Pike). They get away with murdering presidents (one of Color at that) and have been doing their best to stop our rise since their inception. It makes you think about a time in Nazi Germany when propaganda was used to start killing Jews and World War 2 resulted as an effect of that. After the Jews were rescued by every nation that went against Germany, those same Nazi's were brought over to the American government to continue the brutality on the people over here. This was called "Operation Paper Clip". There are 2 things to think about with Nazi Germany: The first is that people came to the rescue of Jews when Hitler was terrorizing them, and a World War came about as a result for helping these Jewish people and stopping the terrorism Hitler was inflicting. Secondly, the same people that terrorized the Jews moved to the wilderness of North America to help these devils over here continue to terrorize us. Some say Hitler and Mussolini borrowed their tactics from the way the white man was treating the so-called Black people over here. They trade tips on how to inflict fear and control on people. How come no one is coming to our rescue and our Holocaust has been going on for over 400 years? Do you get the picture? What is the difference between Nazi Germany and the United States where no one wants to intervene on all the wrong doings this country has done over the years? Just something to think about.

Tell the Truth, Shame the Devil

Chapter 4: The Secret Covenant Review

"An illusion will be so large and so vast it will escape their perception."

For this chapter, I want to discuss a special document that was put out there by the "powers that be" as a guideline on how to maintain power and control over the masses. Sometimes, it's hard to believe that the people that run the world do not have our best interest at heart. Governments were created to run societies and civilizations, but if this is not your culture or civilization, the principles they enforce might be detrimental to your health as an Original man. Now this document is called, "The Secret Covenant" which you can search on Google and find it very easy to show you these people are not keeping their wicked ways a secret from you. They know you will never investigate their agenda because we see white skin as a badge of authority. We feel doctors and scientists with white lab coats are the gospel when it comes to information and would never lie to us to keep this beast of a civilization running. So, we will review this document and I will show you how it is being applied to us on a daily basis with clear examples.

"Those who will see it will be thought of as insane". That's the first sentence to the Secret Covenant and the question I have to ask you as the reader is: how many times have people called you crazy for sharing the truth and knowledge on how we are conditioned and controlled? They have the masses so brainwashed that when you present them with the truth, it is better to shut down than accept it. This is the only society where ignorance is bliss. In ancient times, we would say ignorance is evil.

"We will create separate fronts to prevent them from seeing the connection between us. We will behave as if we are not connected to keep illusion alive". Now, we know when it comes to politics, the opposing parties are 2 wings of the same bird. No matter who you vote for, you are still voting for the same person overall because no matter who is elected as a president, he still has to follow the orders of the elite and powers that be. Matter of fact, John Kerry and George W. Bush are blood cousins and they both ran for presidency at the same time even though they are both part of the same family. This means that it does not matter who wins, they both have the same family agenda. Even Barack Obama and George W. Bush are distant cousins. Researchers of the New England Historic Genealogical Society said, Obama can call six U.S presidents his cousins. They include Bush Junior and Senior, Ford, Johnson, Truman, and James Madison. They found out that he is also related to Churchill. Obama and Bush are linked by Samuel Hinkley of Cape Cod. So, these people bread within their bloodline to be in power with the positions they hold. This makes me think about all those poor American children who want to be a president one day.

"We will work together always and will remain bound by blood and secrecy. Death will come to he who speaks". So they will never come out and tell you they are related and are controlled by the 10% elite of the world. These people stay in power by passing down their bloodline. They call themselves the, "Blue Bloods". No matter what, a regular citizen can never become a president. Every president was picked, not elected by the people. We still think casting votes makes a difference in this society but that goes to show you how powerful the mind control and brainwashing really is.

"We will keep their lifespan short and their minds weak while pretending to do the opposite. We will use our knowledge of science and technology in subtle ways so they will never see what is happening. We will use soft metals, aging accelerators and sedatives in food and water, and also in the air. They will be blanketed by poisons everywhere they turn." When I first read about the information about the "powers that be" keeping our life span short, a statement resonated with me. That statement came from Umar Johnson who said, "If you die before the age of 60, you were murdered." Now-a-days, even making it to the age of 60 is an accomplishment. In ancient times, we use to live for centuries. In this society, getting cancer is so common that we think we're born with it in our genetics. This allows us to disregard blaming our cancer on our poor diet as a factor.

The life span is so low and short in this society that most adults don't want to be adults. Most parents (these days) compete with their children for youthfulness and cool points but subconsciously, we equate adulthood or old age with death instead of life and experience. Everything we consume with the 5 senses affects our mind either positively or negatively. Most of our people's minds are weakened by all the poison and GMO's added to foods we consume. The sad part is that most of us know that fast food causes disease in the body but still eat it. This is a perfect example of being brainwashed and conditioned. Eating

McDonalds or Burger King is an indication of addiction to the chemicals in the food. Research has shown that the meat in the burgers is not coming from cows.

When you know better, you do better. Any time we consciously do something negative, we must come to the conclusion that we are mentally-ill or addicted to the behavior we engage in. Either way, it proves that YOU ARE NOT IN CONTROL. The first law of nature is self-preservation. Nothing in nature destroys itself unless it is manipulated to do so. We are living in a time where if it isn't instant gratification, it's not important. The "powers that be" give you enough poison to make you live until you are 50 or 60 (if you are lucky). You won't know you are being poisoned until you reach an age ranging from 30-40 years. High blood pressure, hair loss, cancer, and accelerated aging are manifestations of poor health.

I have seen a child age 5 grossly obese and just felt sad that her mom (who was also grossly obese) would pass on her mind frame and condition to her daughter and not even know it. Our first years of programming come from our parents and what they allow that baby to digest with the 5 senses. That's why knowledge is key. The powers that be are using knowledge and technology in subtle ways to keep us asleep. Right now, it's hard to find food that hasn't been manipulated by a scientist. Our children today do not know what real food is. They've been consuming chemicals disguised as food, bringing down their health every time they eat. The European is playing "god" with our food, crossing genes of animals with fruits and vegetables to create an affordable product that hides the poison effectively. Let's be real: as long as it's a fruit or vegetable, you won't be as suspicious compared to meats and canned goods.

"The soft metals will cause them to lose their minds. We will promise to find a cure from our many fronts, yet we will feed them more poison. The poisons will be absorbed through their skin and mouths. They will destroy their minds and reproductive systems. From all this, their children will be born dead, and we will conceal this information."

If you look up in the sky on a nice day, you can count on seeing a plane dumping pounds of chemicals into the atmosphere and we never question what it is they are spraying and why they are doing it. Some of the chemicals being sprayed include: Barium, Nano aluminum-coated fiberglass (CHAFF), radioactive Thorium, Cadmium, Chromium, Nickel, Desiccated Blood, Mold Spores, Yellow Fungal Mycotoxins, Ethylene Dibromide, and Polymer Fibers just to name a few. After reading the Secret Covenant, you can see all the soft metals they are spraying in the air and may wonder why most people act like they have lost their minds for real. It's not an act: people have genuinely lost their mind and have a fear for the truth because they have been programed to shut down when something shakes their reality. How many years has cancer research been looking and searching for the cure for cancer and still come up with nothing? No progress has been made in finding a cure for cancer (although it seems like people are getting cancer more frequently).

I know men and women who have personally cured cancer on a number of patients and have records to prove it. Dr. Sebi was sued by the U.S. and won the case because he brought in the people he healed and showed their before and after results after he treated them. Things like diabetes and heart disease should not be running wild the way it is in our people. Part of the reasons for our ailments is due to the slave food we were forced to eat when we were captured by the European and brought to the North American Wilderness.

'Til this day, the European has and will never tell you that the diet we live off of right now was made for slaves, not for free people. In fact, the cure for all diseases can be found in your diet and mind frame. Food should be our medicine. There are no excuses for getting sick in the 21st century with all the health information on the Internet.

The powers that be will never find a cure for AIDS and Cancer because they make too much money off of people dying from taking the drugs used to treat the disease. People don't die from AIDS, they die from the medicine the doctor prescribes to keep the HIV or AIDS under control. Why would anyone pump radioactive substances in their body as a cure? Wouldn't that make them sicker in the end? When people lose their hair, it is a sign of being around radiation for too long. Losing your hair is a sign of disease.

The global pharmaceutical market brings in 300 billion dollars a year in U.S currency. I'm pretty sure the powers that be are not trying to lose that 300 billion dollars to save people because their god is money. Nothing else can save them or make them happier. It makes me wonder where the money really goes when people donate to research and study cases. All of these research institutes are used as fronts to get people's money. None of them are really successful in making breakthroughs in the medical field. The only breakthrough they have is prescribing the latest drug to kill you off faster than the last drug they had.

Miscarriages and STD's are on the rise. This is because parents are not educated on how to care for their body when bringing in another soul into this earth realm.

Abortion clinics are on the rise because this society is governed by the lower urges of lust and sex. They were originally made for so-called Black people to keep our population under control. They called this program, "Planned Parenthood" also known as Eugenics. Abortions increase the mother's chances of having a miscarriage or failed pregnancy. Even if the pregnancy is successful, we normally dumb down our own children by giving them all these vaccinations to "protect them" from this world that the Most High created.

Most women choose not to breastfeed their children for selfish reasons. This inhibits the growth of the baby's brain and throws off their balance until they are old enough to eat solid foods.

We also cheat our children of their maximum potential when we send them to school to be dumbed down and programmed. Our children never come back home the same after they attend public school. If we don't work on deprogramming them and re-educating them when they get home, they will stray and connecting with them will be difficult. The body cannot live without the mind. If the mind is dead, the body can be used by someone else to fulfill their agenda.

"The poison will be hidden in everything that surrounds them, in what they drink, eat, breathe and wear. We must be ingenious in dispensing the poisons for they can't see far. We will teach them that the poisons are good, with fun images and musical tones. Those they look up to will help. We will enlist them to push our poisons." I will add that the poison is even in what you hear and see. Notice how it says they will use people we look up to, to promote their agenda and poison.

Now, think of every music star and film actress in the wilderness of North America. Notice that they only promote the mundane aspects of this society. The most successful artist never has anything intelligent to say. The music industry tries to keep the music at a 4th or 5th grade level to keep us dumb. Most of the rap music out is really a person repeating a negative mantra to program our subconscious. Half the things we find interesting as a people come from us trying to mimic an entertainer.

Rappers brag about all the material wealth they have and trick the youth into thinking money, bitches, and clothes are signs of success. They're used to promote Western Civilization by silent coercion. It's either, make some money promoting something that seems innocent, or put truth in your music and never be heard by the masses. These entertainers are agents for this society and don't work for your best interest. The Jews own all the record labels and exploit as much as they can from these naive artists who just want to be seen and heard by any means necessary.

50 Cent said he was going to, "Get Rich Or Die Trying". How come he wasn't trying to get free or die trying? Most of these entertainers are slaves to the money and industry. They have to keep up with a lifestyle and image they really can't afford, making it look like they're just as successful as white people.

White people are the gold standard for success in the wilderness of North America because it seems like they don't have to struggle or sell out to get it. Most of the time, when you see a European sitcom on television, you don't even know what kind of job they work but they always seem to have money and time to spend with their friends and family. Any time you see an Original person with a massive amount of money (like Oprah or Jay-Z), best believe they were used to make it seem like so-called Black people are getting somewhere in this society. If we work as hard as Oprah or Jay-Z, one day we can have all the money and success they have. This is false. Even if they didn't start out thinking they would be used, the powers that be can always tell who they can use to sell out the race from who they can't.

Normally, when they can't use someone to sell out, they will simply silence them with rumors and character assassination. These people have satellites orbiting the planet that spy on people daily. These satellites are equipped with crazy cameras and telescopes to keep an eye on people. The technology is so advanced it can count every hair on your head. With that said, I can't believe that they don't know who killed Tupac and Biggie Smalls? There is nothing the global elite does not know because they are the ones controlling everything and calling the shots. When they say they can't find cures for things or can't explain some planetary phenomena, best believe they are hiding something.

How many times have you seen a commercial of your favorite artist endorsing something new that you need in your life? During the 90's, rappers were used in beer commercials to sell 40's. R&B singers were used to promote McDonalds and Burger King. They are really using fun images and music tones to sell destruction to the Original mind of my people. If you've ever watched "The Matrix", notice Agent Smith can turn into anyone that is not unplugged from the matrix. This means that 85% of the masses in society are potential enemies that will defend Western Civilization with their lives without second guessing it.

People sign up for the army every day to fight unrighteous wars started by this devilish society in order to colonize the world and capture other nation's natural resources. Propaganda works best when those who are being manipulated are confident that they are acting on their own free will. So, just know half the things you think you do because it's human is actually a manufactured response created by the society you live in.

"We will focus their attention towards money and material goods so they may never connect with their inner self. We will distract them with fornication, external pleasures and games so they may never be one with the oneness (Most High) of it all. Their minds will belong to us and they will do as we say. If they refuse, we shall find ways to implement mind-altering technology into their lives."

I heard a joke from the Master Teacher, Bobby Hemmitt, that always hit home with me. He said "every nigga is one pay cheque away from selling out". I feel like that is the truest statement I've heard in years. Every time you hear rap music, it's all about getting money. People seem to be obsessed with living beyond their means to acquire material goods we can't afford and do not need. We will invest in rims for our car before we invest in our health. We will buy the most expensive clothes and eat the cheapest food.

Keeping the temple clean connects you to your higher Self because you are what you eat. You absorb the nutrients and energy of the foods you eat. Therefore, if the foods you consume are poison, they will poison the body and the mind will not be able to operate at its full potential. They have us distracted, chasing money, forgetting who we are while becoming the job. They have us slaving for the crumbs they give us while they make millions to keep their corporations and societal norms running. We idolize rappers that flaunt and brag about all the money they have and throw it in our face for not having any. In this society, we're trained to think that if we don't have money, we're not even human. Most people that do have money are too greedy to use it in a way to uplift other people.

Where are our modern Kemetic mystery schools in America? We need more schools that are owned by Original people to teach the children knowledge of Self. This will help build a community and a nation that can fight back against white supremacy on a mass scale. Our schools cannot be funded by our enemies and oppressors because the infamous illuminati member Rockefeller said, "If you fund your enemies, you will destroy them quietly." For the success of education for the children, we must have a separation of righteousness and evil. That means taking a stand and separating from anything that supports Western civilization because anything we do that strengthens this society, strengthens the Secret Covenant they have to hold us down as a people.

We need to start seeing women as sisters, mothers, and wives before we see them as sexual objects because lust is the urge of the lower Self. The honorable Elijah Muhammad always taught that a nation can rise no higher than its women because she is the first teacher of the baby. The baby gets its nutrients and support from the mother for 9 months before birth and years after being born. She raises the child to be strong and carry on the duties of a civilized nation.

We need to stop chasing instant gratification and think about the future ahead. We need to start living below our means - that is the only way you will get ahead in life. When families from the East travel to the West, they normally cram the whole family into one house and pool their money together to run the family business. You normally see 3 generations in one household.

Take Brampton, a city located in Ontario, Canada for instance. The demographics show a strong community of East Indians who own their own grocery stores, restaurants, plazas, temples, schools, and clinics. They can only accomplish that by having a nationality and a culture of their own. They wear their own clothes and eat their own food that they bought from their grocery store. They speak their own language so they can make outsiders know what they want them to know, when they want them to know it.

Chinatown is another good example. They're located in every major city in the wilderness of North America. Other nationalities can maintain a certain lifestyle because they never had their culture taken away from them. They know in order to strive and build, having an economic system that keeps the money in their community is a necessity. They will serve their own people before they serve others because they have a knowledge of who they are and a culture. There is no holocaust like the 400+ year holocaust of the Original man that is still going on as we speak. We are too distracted by mundane things like money. However, any spiritual man knows the war is not over until we win.

"We will use fear as our weapon. We will establish their governments and establish opposites within. We will own both sides. We will always hide our objective but carry out our plan. They will perform the labor for us and we shall prosper from their toil." How many of us are too scared to be ourselves? I once asked my niece why she doesn't wear her hair natural. Her response was, "because it's nappy" or, "I have a sister who had to cut her hair because of all the damage the perms and weaves did and now she wears a wig because she is ashamed she doesn't have long hair". The self-hatred is real and the fear of being Original is even bigger. When you go against nature it will naturally destroy you. There is no way around it.

Fear gets stored in the kidney. Studies show that Original people are dying from ESRD (End Stage Renal Disease) at a higher rate than any other race.

Living in fear and stress is killing our people at an alarming rate. Most diseases are started because of the stressful environment we're living in.

There has never been a time when the U.S. government has served in the people's favor. It has always worked for its own interest because it is a corporation and the military faction for Western Civilization.

This Secret Covenant document really makes me think. Even if it isn't written by the Illuminati, why is it so accurate with everything that is going on in the world? I'll let you decide.

Chapter 5: So-Called Black Consciousness Power

"This society can only operate off of you being outside of your mind".

Amos Wilson said, "We need a change in perception and a change in how we see things as a collective. We need to work our way up from rebellion to revolution to reverse what this society has done to us and bring it back to how we once had it when we were kings and queens."

This is only possible through knowledge of Self. Once you know who you are and what you are capable of, there is nothing that will stop your wisdom and understanding. You will live according to the will of the cosmos.

Now, in order for this society to function, it literally must have its citizens and subjects out of their natural universal mind provided by the Creator. Mind control works best through deception and it is easy for us to be deceived because we trust the source of information and the person deceiving us.

Amos Wilson said, "For us to be in the position we are in, we have to be crazy". His statement makes the most sense when you realize that Original people make up the majority of the planet earth. How could the minority rule the majority (unless the minority knows something the majority does not)? This means the education we receive in this society is not made to liberate us but to perpetuate the already agreed upon lie to further this society.

Right now, we are dealing with the invasion of the body snatchers. We look like Africans but have the mind of Europeans. Ask the average Melinated person about Voodoo and they will most likely say it's "devil worship". Also, dare to speak about wanting equality and justice for our people and they might call you a radical. In fact, the only time the Original man is called "racist" is when he talks about rising out of oppression. When you say you want to liberate your people, the devil will ask about the struggle of other races. When they ask this, they insinuate that other races of people are struggling just as bad as the Original man and womb man around the world. They want you to worry about everyone else's struggle, so that you will have no time for your own.

Melinated people will join forces with the gay agenda, animal rights, or Occupy Wall Street. However, you don't see members of the gay agenda, animal rights, or Occupy Wall Street joining our struggle to fight against white supremacy. It's time for people to rally for the justice of so-called Black people.

There's a huge disconnect when it comes to our people. We feel more sympathy for other people than our own. We identify with the Jewish holocaust more than the African holocaust that took over 100,000,000 African lives in the Trans-Atlantic Slave Trade alone. When we look at every discipline in this society, we are not included in it. We are not a part of the economics of this society except as consumers. They only need us to spend the little bit of money we get from them to support their businesses.

On television, most shows seem like a White man's wonderland or fantasy with minimal positive representation of Original people. It's 2014 and we have never seen a "fantasy" land where it's only so-called Black people living civilized and prominent looking like the mother and fathers of civilization. All these biblical-based movies coming out in theatre are not historically accurate. All the main characters of the movies are White.

Now, if the White man is not the devil, how come he never speaks up when he is wrong? Why would "good white people" allow black people to worship and pray to a White Jesus knowing it is historically impossible for any prophet to ever be white? It's because they are guilt-deficient as a people.

Dr. Francis Cress Welsing once said, "If a white person is truly your friend, ask them what white people say about you when you are not around". We must recognize that the European is a Devil. The same devil in the Bible, Koran, and all folklore and mythology. The definition of a devil means, "deceiver" or "one who deceives". The 10% of the population can't control the other 90% unless the minority has the majority deceived through falsification of information and history. They have us living in a false consciousness where we only make moves and decisions that benefit them and further their agenda. Every institute in this society is made to maintain the status quo of Western civilization and white supremacy. In this society, school is used to keep you dumb; welfare is used to keep you poor; and religion is used to send you to hell.

The justice system turns us into criminals. The psychiatric industry is used to keep us crazy. All this is done in the name of mind control.

The first step in brainwashing is to remove the Original identity and give them a new personality foreign to his/her nature. The 21st century Black man is a European invention. The process of slavery and oppression has turned us into a brand new breed of people. Now, we have a new way of dealing with the world because we are living under different conditions. The brain programs its environment. Therefore, the conditions of the environment live inside of us. When foreign people give you the conditions for our people to live in, they are ultimately trying to create you.

When we look at life and this society, we must compare it to the lab rat and the scientist running experiments on the rat. In school, they never taught you that you were the rat and the government was the scientist running the experiment on you. The relationship between the rat and the experimenter is a political situation. The experimenter has power and the rat is powerless. The scientist puts the rat in any condition he pleases. He feeds you when you complete a task and he will shock you with electricity when you don't complete the task accordingly. This is the perfect example of the Reward-Punishment system, created by B.F Skinner. Applying the same system to this society can help us identify how people's conditions can be manipulated because we do not want to be punished and we don't want to stand out as an outcast. You get outcasted when you teach the realities of what is going on in the world.

We're still celebrating these holidays we have no history on. We are blindly giving our energy away to days and deities we have no knowledge of. For example, Thanksgiving Day is the day Native Americans were deceived and destroyed by the Europeans.

Those who think for themselves know you don't need a special day to be thankful and build with their family. Nothing holy has ever come out of Europe so why would they have holy days? Most of these days are celebrating the victories of white men taking advantage of original people.

For example, St. Patricks Day is really the day the Moors were chased out of Ireland. Moors were known as "Druids" or "Celtic Pagans". Another example is Valentine's Day. Its origins are in Rome, Italy where they celebrate Luperaclia, honoring Faunus (god of fertility) on February 15th. Men would go to a grotto dedicated to Lupercal (the wolf god; located at the foot of Palatine Hill) where Romans believe that the founders of Rome (Romulus and Remus) were suckled by a she-wolf. The men would sacrifice a goat or dog, cut the skin, and run around, hitting women with the hides of the animals they killed.

Personally, if a female I was dating tried to break up with me or gave me a hard time for not celebrating or participating in this holiday, I would automatically know she's been programmed and doesn't know better.

Every day, our behavior is controlled by things we do not know about and make us believe we made the right decision for ourselves.

For instance, summer 2013, the ice bucket challenge went viral to spread awareness of ALS (Amyotrophic Lateral Sclerosis). Turns out this sickness doesn't affect Melinated people. Why are so-called Black people raising money and awareness for a disease that has nothing to do with them?

Melinated people suffer from a disease called sickle cell that only Melinated people get and apparently has no cure. Why aren't we doing ice bucket challenges to raise the awareness of sickle cell? White people aren't raising awareness for sickle cell because it doesn't affect them. Again, what is it with our people that we identify with the struggles of everyone else but our own?

Overall, we have been under the authority of the White man. We are hypnotized by his power. A technique for hypnotizing a subject is to command him or her to do something you want. If they respect your authority enough, they will go into a hypnotic trance. The people who lie to us the most are the people we are the quickest to believe. In fact, we don't believe it until they say it. White skin is the symbol of authority in this society. This perception will only change once we stop externalizing our power to a system that exists to destroy us.

Chapter 6: The Wake Up Call

It is a political necessity to keep Melinated people dumb and out of their mind. If we were to wake up to what is really going on, the people in power will not be in power anymore. In the meantime, concentration camps and military forces are not needed to control us. There is already enough psychological warfare that is going on. We cannot be servants to the oppressor and keep our roots because everything about this society is anti-African. By serving this society and being subject to acculturation, we ultimately destroy ourselves.

Right now, we are witnessing a willingness to destroy ourselves in order to win the favor and reward of those controlled by white people. We are criticized when we are not up to date with the latest fashion and shoes. Everything about us has become very materialistic and that is because we have the mind of the devil and the devil is materialistic. He works off of appearance so he can deceive you.

The word, "devil" simply means to deceive. There are no bigger deceivers on the planet earth than the people who created and support Western Civilization. This is a parasitic culture that leaves its citizens in a, "crabs-in-a-bucket mentality" to get ahead. It's built on keeping people down to stay on top. It's like a massive pyramid scheme.

Presently, in the 21st century, we are making the devils job really easy. We are making it so easy to the point where it seems like his hands are clean. Perpetuating the facade that so-called Blacks are killing so-called Blacks. But who orchestrates the factors that lead to these fatalities.

My father once told me, "Black people have done more wrong to themselves than white people". It has always disturbed me how much love he has for white people. My father is one of many obedient slaves to Western Civilization. At the same time, I cannot blame him because any education he ever received came from White people. Any form of money he earned came from White people. He believes that Jesus, Adam, and Eve are White. Every aspect of his life is dependent on white people to the point where if something doesn't come from the white man, it can't be true.

I know many people like my father who complain and ask, "When will black people get it together?". However, they don't seem to notice the underlying theme of white supremacy in the lives of Original people. Situations like this demonstrate that society is one big brainwashing campaign. How can you make it to old age without knowing the truth? Lies can only be true when they are agreed upon by many. Numbers reinforce confidence in people when it comes to support.

For instance, the cop that killed Mike Brown had supporters that raised over $200,000 dollars for his cause because this society rewards people that try to destroy us. Many of us are living life according to lies we agree upon consciously, subconsciously, or unconsciously. The belief in these lies can easily be reversed if we just asked questions and embarked on self-education. We are living in the age of the World Wide Web where everything is one Google away.

There is no excuse to still be blind to the truth (unless something is distracting you or keeping you from caring). In nature, self-perseveration is the order of the day to things with intelligence.

The mass ritual trauma that the Original man and woman have been subjected to for over 400 years has us doing anything to get rid of the pain. The Trans-Atlantic slave trade was one big trauma based program ritual to turn Gods into Niggers. People who are traumatized by abuse at a young age end up in abusive relationships when they get older. That is what we have now. Post-Traumatic Slave Disorder is a phenomenon where Original people can't let go of what the White man has taught us through slavery. It's as if we weren't given anything to reverse the spell.

For example, in this society, we aren't taught how to properly eat to live. Around the world, different cultures have their own national dishes and foods they eat to survive. If we travelled up North, the Inuit eat raw seal and whale meat to survive. In other regions of the world, people eat more vegetables to survive. Fried chicken and pigs feet are the scraps the master didn't want, so we turned it into a delicacy.

The White man used to wear fur coats because they didn't bathe and the ticks that were on their bodies would jump into their coat. Now, we turned wearing fur into a fashion statement.

Picnics or barbecues were invented by White people to find a slave to lynch, burn, amputate, and cannibalize him. They have recipe books on how to cook and season a so-called Black man's penis to this day. It's obvious we're suffering from Stockholm syndrome. Stockholm syndrome is a psychological phenomenon in which a hostage expresses positive feelings toward their captors (sometimes to the point of defending and identifying with them). These feelings are irrational.

Now, let's analyze the Stockholm syndrome in the wilderness of North America. During slavery, we were robbed of our language, culture, religion, human rights, and reduced to cattle. The slave masters viewed us as subhuman. We labored and did all the hard work to build and fight for this country and still weren't given equal rights. They had white only water fountains, schools, and designated seats on the bus. Instead of separating and building our own African-centered businesses, we fought for integration. We try to be more colonized than the colonizer. Whenever we point out the wrong doings of Western civilization, the mentally enslaved come to the defense of the colonizer. It's hard to even get Black people to admit that white supremacy exists. We are quick to fight for the rights of homosexuals, join feminists, and dumping buckets of waters on our head for ASL. When it comes down to others joining the so-called Black man and woman's struggle, it never happens. Whenever there has been a world war on the planet, so-called Black people have always been happy to join and fight a fight that has nothing to do with them. Any so-called Black man in the U.S. army should be ashamed of themselves because they are serving in the devil's army. It is irrational to think that Western civilization has anything beneficial to give the so-called Black man in the wilderness of North America and the only reason we think otherwise is because we are brainwashed and conditioned to believe so. This is why a true revolution starts in the mind. We must give the devil his mind back and take back the mind of the Original man.

The success in them controlling us so well falls down to fear and trauma based programming. Fear is keeping us from being the best we can be. No one can operate at full potential under constant fear. That is why, for instance, the news broadcasted on television is never positive. There's always bad news about terrorists, plane crashes, and viruses breaking out. Many live their life according to the news. If the news doesn't report something, it's considered to be obsolete or not important. For instance, a news report will caution the masses of the dangers of the flu and encourage vaccination. Mercury is the main poison put into these vaccinations to keep your life span short and your mind dumbed down.

Fear keeps one from thinking rationally. Many have fell for the "end of the world" hoax, buying up food and rations for survival only to find out they have been tricked. Some religious cults will make people sell everything to gain salvation while the pulpit pimp lives a luxurious lifestyle. Religion is another mass brainwashing machine to make you look outside of your Self for a savior. You will externalize your power to a mystery God and live in hell thinking there is a heaven to go to after your suffering. As long as you believe your happiness and fate is in the hands of an outside source, you will always lead a life of suffering. The government funds and protects churches because it is one of the tools it uses to keep people dumb, deaf, and blind. Fear makes you externalize your power so you will start looking for strength in other people. We should look to ourselves to change our condition.

Trauma and abuse can induce multi-personality disorder/dissociative behavior. The mind builds amnesia walls so it doesn't have to relive the moment of trauma, causing the formation of a different person. This can be seen when the Original man disconnects from his roots because of the trauma endured through slavery. This makes the Original man only feel successful when he has European acquisition (like Nike shoes named after a Greek god of victory). Rappers never rap about the African acquisition.

Even sisters wear weaves and wigs to hide their natural kinky hair. I asked my niece why she wears a weave and her reasons were to conceal her "Nigger naps". So-called Black women are the only people who wear other people's hair to hide their own. The so-called Black hair care industry is a half a trillion dollar ($500,000,000,000) market and Melinated people make no profit. No so-called Black owned products are sold in Korean hair and nail shops. This means all our money goes to outside communities as soon as we get it. If so-called Black women stopped doing their hair for one year, we would be a strong half a trillion dollar nation. Think about how positively our economics would be affected if we invested in ourselves.

Sometimes, you have to live below your means in order to move forward but some people are too proud to struggle. We would rather look like we are doing well than actually work at being good. There are people in this world with no shoes and all the joy in the world. On the flip side, we are worried about owning every Jordan's sneaker that comes out but we never ask what Michael Jordan has done for the so-called Black community. He is very wealthy but hasn't built an African-centered school. That can either be because he doesn't have knowledge of self or he's not allowed to. Either way, it means he's not in control. The same thing can be said about Oprah. She gives her crowd new cars and build schools in Africa. However, if these schools are teaching the curriculum of the devil, it's not helping to advance the welfare of Original people. The curriculum of the devil breeds another generation of brainwashed people ready to keep Europeans in power.

The African-centered curriculum should consist of teachings by the likes of Ivan Van Sertima, Dr. Afrika, Ra Un Nefer, and Muata Ashby that teach: the history of the Original man's civilization in times of antiquity; how a body full of melanin responds to certain foods; ancient Kemetic sciences/languages, etc. A weak body can't support a strong mind. There is no point in having knowledge and not put it into practice. We knew how to govern ourselves and the planet for millions of years. We do not need another race of people to teach and push their agenda on us.

Moorish Americans can trace their flag back 10,000 years. The Washitah tribe can trace their history in North America over 50,000 years. Therefore, for us to be following a people that has only been here for 6000 years (2000 of which they were living in caves like a savage) demonstrates how much power we've externalized as a people. We've been conned out of our wealth, land, and mind. The minority has gained control over the majority. They control our consciousness as a people. A "Nigga" is a White man's invention and most of our people are proud Niggas right now. We have the fourth highest spending power in the world. Therefore, we aren't poor. We just need to organize and galvanize our resources to create our own economy. Even the music industry is worth billions and we accept pennies for record deals.

I recently read a September 2014 article about Keke Palmer being the first "African-American" woman to play Cinderella on Broadway. To me, it's just pitiful how she's celebrated for something that's approved by the white man. What is up with wanting to drink from the white only fountain? Why didn't she create her own Cinderella play with all so-called Black people and make it relatable to our people? Or better yet: why not tell the story of African queens in times of antiquity? The only time Melinated people feel they made it is when a white man recognizes them. White people are the gold standard of success in this society.

Overall, once the majority unites under one African banner of unity around the world, we will take back our rightful position on the planet earth within a day. The white man can't save us even if we were to teach him about his past and who he is. Every time we accepted him amongst us, he took advantage and tricked us with his forked tongue and double speech. They take from other cultures and murder out of survivors. For example, the Europeans couldn't go to space without exploiting the Mother Land because they spray the space equipment with melanin. Even the silicon and crystals in the electronics come from the Mother Land. Whoever controls Africa controls the world as a whole. We need to get back to our original mind and unite. This is the only way to drive out the Western mind out of Africa and the wilderness of North America.

Chapter 7: The Engineering of Consent

For this chapter, I want to concentrate on the history of propaganda in America and how it has been used to control the masses to manufacture responses in people.

The first concept I will discuss is called the Engineering of Consent. It is when the powers that be make you think you are making your own choices but have manipulated your subconscious forces to think you need the things you want. Most commercials and advertisements are looked over by a psychoanalyst to see how the human mind will react before they put it on air. In the music industry, music videos and singles are picked out by a psychoanalyst but they are disguised as the personal relations agent (PR). The PR agent is responsible for promoting your singles and videos and giving you advice on what to do next for your next move.

For instance, they advise female artists to be more sexually suggestive or make controversial statements in interviews. Most entertainers do not live the life they portray in their music videos. Most are not as rich as you think. In fact, they are just as much at risk as the average person living a 9-5 to poverty if they don't sell. As soon as these entertainers' careers are over, they are left with nothing because they spent their money keeping up with an extravagant lifestyle they can't afford.

The man who invented the portrayal of extravagant lifestyles that advertise other brands and corporations is Edward Bernays. He is dubbed, "The Father of Propaganda" and the nephew of Sigmund Freud who is dubbed, "The Father of Psychoanalysis". Bernays taught American corporations how to make Americans want things they didn't need by linking mass produced goods to their unconscious desires. Bernays' and Freuds' theories on human behavior are widely accepted in this society as truth and taught in every school in Western civilization. They believe human beings have an irrational, dangerous, and instinctive animal-like drive. This kind of drive has been attributed to the cause of Word War 1 and considered strong enough to cause mobs powerful enough to overthrow governments.

When America was going to war, they created the Committee of Public Information and hired Bernays to promote what was going on overseas in the war to the press. They used Bernays' propaganda to promote the restoration of the Old Empire and democratize Europe. "Making the world safe through democracy" was the slogan he came up with. When Bernays accompanied President Woodrow Wilson to a peace conference in Paris, France, his propaganda portrayed President Wilson as a liberator of the people and a man concerned with the free will of man partaking in the politics of its country. He looked like a hero to the public eye and Bernays had the idea to use this kind of propaganda after the war during times of peace in America. After the war, Bernays started The Council On Public Relations because Hitler used the propaganda to assist in the Holocaust of Jews and gave the word a bad rep.

Bernays started studying the works of his uncle, Freud, regarding the irrational forces in humans. His studies fascinated him to the point where he started looking into monetizing it by manipulating the unconscious. Bernays works are the foundation of modern day propaganda. He pretty much turned the masses into consumers.

His first successful experiment was getting women to smoke cigarettes. The cigarette industry came to Bernays and said they are losing half their market to the taboo that women shouldn't smoke in public. So Bernays and a group of psychoanalysts came to the conclusion that if they could connect cigarettes with the idea of challenging male power. In New York, at an Easter Day parade, Bernays staged a protest with a bunch of young rich females who had cigarettes and started smoking. He then informed the press that a group of fearless women were smoking cigarettes to demonstrate their power. After this demonstration, the sales in cigarettes sky rocketed and made Bernays an instant success with American corporations. Bernays created the image and idea that if a woman smoked, it made her look more powerful, independent, and equal to men. In Bernays mind, this confirmed that if you linked products to people's emotions and feelings, you can make them act irrational.

Whites allowing so-called Black people to spend money in, "Whites-only" stores made so-called Black people stop spending money in their own communities. This caused the White man to get richer. Any intelligent human being would classify this behavior as irrational and can be used as a proper diagnosis for mental illness.

Self-preservation is the first law of nature. Original people in the wilderness of North America attacked by propaganda, forcing conformity to societal norms is a sign that we are under mind control. Just like how Bernays made White women feel powerful by smoking cigarettes, they made so-called Black people feel more equal by not lynching them, allowing them to vote, and spending money out of their community.

This is how they sold the American dream. However, it is really a nightmare for Black people. When a sales man sells a product, he doesn't sell it to your intellect. He sells it to your emotions and feelings.

For example, you might not need new clothes but buying new clothes feels good. Also, a car sales man may let you test drive a car and ask how it feels. As Bernays success started to rise, he was hired by corporations. He taught them how to trick people into buying products by studying what motivates the human mind.

An owner of a woman's magazine hired Bernays to promote his magazine. He glamorized the magazine by placing ads and articles of famous film stars wearing certain products he wanted to promote. He invented product placement, he is the reason why to this day companies will send rappers and famous entertainer's clothes and products to wear in their music videos. He is also used to employ psychologists to issue reports praising a product, pretending they were tested in independent studies. This is where myths like drinking milk make your bones stronger come from. He is the reason the FDA can promote poison as health products because they give the public fraudulent results for test they never did.

When Freud was going bankrupt, Bernays sent him money so he could publish his books in America. They went on a campaign to make sure any and every one had a copy of the book. Today, Freud's books have an enormous impact on American intellectuals. They were really fascinated with the picture he painted of group behavior.

Freud changed the way government and politicians saw the masses. This way of thinking breeded what we know as "elitism". It is when a group of people want to control you because they think you are not smart enough to make your own decisions. Walter Lipmen once said, "If human beings are in reality driven by unconscious irrational forces, then it is necessary to rethink democracy. What we need is a new elite to manage the bewildered herd". Through the eyes of elites, the masses are seen as useless eaters who need to be controlled or removed.

What people don't know is that democracy is married to capitalism. It is impossible to have one without the other. Democracy and capitalism mean that every home in America must have a television so you can receive their messages of brainwashing. They just so happen to make you pay for that brainwashing by sending you a cable bill every month. They make sure every household has a microwave oven to absorb radiation in the body when you eat your food. Every household has running water with just enough fluoride to drive people crazy and then send you a hydro bill for using their poisonous water. In reality, we are not in charge of anything and democracy does not exist anywhere else on this planet earth.

Original people in the wilderness of North America desire to be seen as equal to white people. They want the same status and power as white people because white people don't get brutalized by police officers nor suffer during the Atlantic slave trade.

We are so traumatized and manipulated as a people that we are willing to take on traits of the devil just to get ahead in life. This is exactly what they want us to do. They want us to conform to this society. Conforming to this society means throwing away anything that connects you back to who you really are as an Original man or woman. The result of conforming to this society and losing the connection of who you are always results in mental illness and anxiety.

Anna Freud had subjects that she trained and raised since they were children and they all suffered mental break downs in adulthood. Some committed suicide and some became raging alcoholics and drug addicts.

Right now, if you look at the world, you will see it is nothing but madness going on. You have police brutality at an all-time high and wars constantly breaking out in the Middle East. There is supposedly an Ebola epidemic and the cure that doctors have created can only cure people with pale skin. The ISIS terrorist group that is all funded by America.

America gives both sides of the war arms and lets them destroy each other in order to generate fear in people. Only someone under mind control would join the U.S army and go around the world killing innocent people. Bernays' propaganda techniques are used to make people believe there is a threat to America's security and that defense is needed to keep its citizens safe. However, Western civilization is the true threat.

Western civilization mass produces death no matter where it goes in the world. Three quarters of the planet has received its guns and artillery from America. In 2012, the United States made 73 billion dollars from selling arms to different nations around the world. They even have a 10 billion dollar deal with Saudi Arabia and the United Arab Emirates. All so called terrorist groups are funded by the United States and the C.I.A. because the C.I.A. was created to undermine all governments. In 2009, the arms market in the United States made 31 billion dollars. In 2012, the budget for U.S. defense was 656 billion dollars. There was rise in sales of arms in the U.S. from 2009 to 2012 and it's only going to get higher.

Now let's take the time to brain storm how 656 billion dollars could change the world for everyone's benefits. That amount of money could stop world hunger for generations. It could make sure everyone's basic needs are met. The money isn't even used on the tax payers of America. You have homelessness, unemployment, and the need for welfare at an all-time high. It's almost like America wants to fix the world's problems before it fixes the problems it has at home. Thanks to Freud, the global elite think it's necessary to manipulate the inner feelings of the American population. As long as you are governed by fear, you will look outside yourself for immediate solutions and this society always has a solution for a problem it created.

When Freud and Bernays were referring to irrational behaviors in human beings, they were really speaking to Europeans. The Original man is born righteous by nature. He has gone thousands of years living under love, truth, peace, freedom, justice. The United States of America is only 238 years old and has been in countless amounts of war. This country has never known peace. It has always been involved in bloodshed and benefiting off of the work of other people and they have tricked you into thinking it is ok. You wouldn't participate in the madness if you really knew better.

Conforming to this society has so-called Black women acting like white feminists. Throughout the history of the White man, he has never had respect for his woman. That's why you see cartoons of him as a cave man hitting his woman over the head with a piece of wood or a rock and then dragging her into the caves. Women have always been secondary in Western civilization. That's why you have such a high rate of homosexuality in their society. The reason we live in a patriarchal system is because of Western civilization. In a patrilineal system, woman are raped and had to bring the dowry.

When you have a relationship in this society, you become the property of your mate. In ancient African culture, the matrilineal system was used as a way to exalt women. We always sent praise to the woman and seen her as equal or superior to us. We say we came from the Cosmic Womb, call the planet we live on Mother Earth, and abide by the rules of Mother

Nature. You never see a God without a Goddess in ancient times because they were always teaching the universal law of gender and polarity. We are programmed to treat each other the same way the Europeans treat everybody. The Europeans do not see things as equal. They like to separate things because it makes it easier for them to have control.

In the 1950's, the C.I.A. poured millions of dollars into the psychology departments of universities across America. They were secretly funding experiments on how to alter and control the inner drives of human beings. That means these people spend millions of dollars to take advantage of you and keep you out of knowing what is really going on in the world.

Overall, propaganda was invented to persuade the deciding factors in your mind. People perish from a lack of knowledge. Getting the information from the right information source is needed to make informed decisions at all times. As long as the powers that be have you thinking that you're making your own decisions, they have you right where they want you.

Chapter 8: Funds & Cover Ups

This society is one big social experiment to see how much money the "powers that be" can make while keeping 85 percent of the population in the dark about who they really are.

Nowadays, people are so brainwashed that they are willing participants to the madness. Even bringing up the war on so-called Black people will cause you to be viewed as a conspiracy theorist. Some may think it is a conspiracy theory that crack cocaine was pumped into so-called Black communities all over the U.S. When different groups like the Nation of Islam came to the rescue, infiltrators like the Anti-Defamation League made sure they stopped them from saving lives, in order to make money to fund other wars around the world.

A number of former C.I.A. agents came out with details as to how they helped bring drugs into this country. Even when the White man comes out confessing what he has done to Original people, we can't believe that he would do such a thing because he is the gold standard of society.

This government has brought over war criminals from the Nazi camp to continue the terrorism of Original people around the world in Operation Paper Clip. After Operation Paper Clip, the U.S. government applied teachings from the Nazis by starting Eugenics programs aimed at killing so-called Black people by forced sterilization. They justify their actions by saying some people are born with inferior genes and must be eliminated in order to build a healthy nation and country.

This society has funded dangerous and inhumane programs like M.K ultra where they gave people drugs and shock treatment without the consent of the people. They have ruined thousands of lives by removing parts of their brains that connect them to the memory of their past, leaving them empty and with a changed personality.

Even for you to join the U.S army means you joined the devils army, thinking you are fighting for your country. The army is a brainwashing camp and the education system was set up by the military. Right now, the U.S. government is funding Israel in all its endeavors to murder people.

Furthermore, the police force are bandits who have no jurisdiction over you if you are an Original man or Moorish American. In ancient times, we didn't have prisons because we were not criminals. We viewed criminality as a mental illness that must have come from somewhere foreign.

In the area of social engineering, John B. Watson used to experiment on babies to find out which race was superior. The Rockerfeller's also played a big role in the advancement of social engineering between 1922 and 1929. The Rockerfeller Foundation gave out almost 50 million dollars for the pursuit of social sciences around the world. They set out to change society as a whole and started the Yale Institute of Human Relations. The Rockerfellers gave the Yale Institute of Human Relations 7 million dollars to study social science. The secret society, Skull and Bones, operates out of Yale University as well (in which George Bush is a member of).

An example of the working class being turned into human robots is in Ford's introduction of the assembly line to the industrial factories in the United States. Work was fragmented so that one person did a task. By fragmenting the work, you just had to do what you were told when you were told to do it without needing to know the whole operation.

Western civilization would end in 24 hours if everybody decided not to go to work. This society is so devilish that if everyone really did decide not to go to work, they would call in the military and the army to force us to work.

They commit acts like this out of fear. They are so scared that they are killing Original people to avoid genetic annihilation because they have recessive genes.

Unfortunately, we have been taught to view freedom by the standard of Western civilization. For instance, there have been cures for cancer and proof that AIDS doesn't kill people. We're dying from curable diseases because the powers that be conceal the cures from us. They keep away holistic practitioners such as Dr. Sebi because he has cured many diseases for over 20 years. In 2011, 954 billion dollars was made off of not having a cure for anything. It always falls back to money with Western civilization. Everything about Western civilization is materialistic. That's why they go and conquer other lands to control the natural resources that fuel this society. Computers and all electronics wouldn't exist if it wasn't for Africa because that's where they extract the material from. What's ironic is that they don't allow Africans to have the same technology because then they would have competition and less control over the resources.

Dr. Umar Johnson said it best: "Whoever controls Africa controls the world". That means if the world is run by White supremacy, that they're invaders on our land. These invaders exploit our resources and also cause famine, disease, and war. Every third-world country is either a country that went into debt after taking IMF funds or didn't take funds from the IMF and can't do business with countries indebted to the IMF.

A devil once said: "I care not who writes the laws as long as I control the money". This statement means when you own money, you can hire people to create laws that work in your favor. This system was not made for us to be successful. It was made for us to keep them successful unknowingly. They have the power to redefine sin and legitimize their misbehavior.

Most of the problems Original people face stem from powerlessness and lack of knowledge of Self. The European does what he does because he can get away with it. No one ever questions anything Western civilization does and 85 percent don't even notice that something is wrong with this civilization. This society is pathological, crazy, and fueled by everything opposite of love, truth, peace, freedom, and justice. They take advantage of us every chance they get. We can reverse this once we get back to our original frame of mind.

Tell the Truth, Shame the Devil

Chapter 9: Methods & Techniques

For this chapter, I want to go into some of the techniques that are used in this society to keep the masses brainwashed and under mind control. I've noticed that when the subject of mind control comes up in a conversation, people speak as if it can't happen to them or they haven't been brainwashed already. We see mind control and hypnotism as a spinning wheel with a spiral in the middle but it is much deeper than that.

The U.S. has developed technology that can look into the human brain and read our thoughts. Their technology utilizes Gigahertz (GHZ), radiation, and extra low frequencies (ELF) which allow them to convey commands to a subject that sound like voices in the subject's head.

Soviet scientists in Russia have been using this technology since 1934. They found out that when minute currents of electromagnetic energy are introduced into the brain, profound changes occur. Scientists have been able to create addictive behavior in people by shocking and stimulating certain parts of the brain. By the 1970's, Russian scientists have perfected their technology to be better at keeping the masses under mind control. Their advances have allowed them to create implants, microchips, electrodes, and drugs through the use of microwave, radio waves, and electromagnetic energy. By applying these methods, the eternal brain waves (EEG) are able to be entrained.

It has been demonstrated and proven that direct transfer of information to the brain could be carried out through radio frequency waves modulated at levels that are non-lethal. When electromagnetic signals are tailored at certain frequencies, they cannot be stopped and the subject has no choice but to receive the message. The message could be anything from shooting up a school, movie theatre, or assassinating a president. Physical control of different brain functions have been demonstrated facts in various experiments. It is even possible to follow the intentions and development of thought through visual experiences.

The C.I.A. has spent billions of dollars and found different techniques for controlling the masses. They have hired scientists from all around the world to conduct secret experiments on unsuspecting people. When Ronald Reagan was elected into office, he created the National Security Agency (NSA). They were created to devise ways of dealing with threats to the White House.

On March 30 1981, Reagan left the Hilton Hotel and a man by the name of John Hinckley started to fire shots aimed at him. Although he was aiming for Reagan, Hinckley wounded: police officer, Thomas Delahanty; secret service agent, Timothy McCarthy; and critically wounded press secretary, James Brady. Hinckley did not hit Reagan directly, but seriously wounded him with a bullet that ricocheted off the side of the presidential limousine. That bullet ended up hitting him in the chest. John Hinckley did not attempt to flee the scene after he fired the shots and was arrested immediately. When police investigated Hinkley's motif, they found out he committed the crime because he was told to do it. Now, my question is: why didn't he run? Why would he follow random orders to kill just because someone told him to? Evidence points to him being hypnotized at the time of his capture. June 21 1982, Hinckley was found not guilty by reason of insanity and was confined to the St. Elizabeth Hospital in Washington, DC. He received special treatment by being able to visit his parents periodically and not being allowed to speak to news media about his life.

The reason why I am using Hinkley's attempted murder on Reagan as an example is because I find it strange that he was treated so well for trying to take the president's life. While he was in the mental hospital, they ran various tests and experiments on him and kept everything a secret from the public. Another interesting fact is that Hinckley's father was a financial supporter of George H. W. Bush's 1980 presidential campaign. Scott Hinckley, John Hinckley's brother, had a dinner date with the Vice President's son, Neil Bush, the day after the assassination attempt.

One technique that was made popular by Dr. Milton H. Erickson (a psychiatrist specializing in medical hypnosis) was called the Confusion-Hypnosis technique. This technique induces a trance like state on the mind. It works by giving the targeted person so much to deal with in an ultra-short period of time so that he has no time to deal with anything on his own. One thing after another is thrown at the subject, constantly shifting their focus until the subject shows signs of collapse or about to break. At this moment, the hypnotist provides some relief and instructions that comfort the subject into a trance.

On May 24th 1984, the *Miami Herald* ran an article on a man named James P. He was a former C.I.A. pilot and claimed to be a victim of the same agency he worked for. James was certain that he had been given a mind control implant while he was a patient at the U.S. Army Institution of Surgical Research in San Antonio, Texas. The alleged date he received this implant was on April 1982. The hospital records show that James did not leave the hospital until July 2nd, 1982. He maintained that he was being subjected to mind control with an X-ray proving an implant right behind the left ear. Once he saw the X-Ray, he immediately contacted the media and told reporters he suspected that the C.I.A was going to use him to assassinate someone. He urged the media to check suspects who attempted to assassinate politicians and leaders for mind control implants. His warning came from suspecting that men like Lee Harvey Oswald, Sirhan Sirhan, and John Hinckley were victims of covert specific programming.

The purpose of mind altering techniques is you can produce a state of consciousness in a person where they will carry out any wish at your command. No one will ever know you had a hand in it because most of the time, the subject's memory is wiped out or weakened.

Implants and chips are not needed anymore because they have radio waves that can transfer thoughts right into your head. The global elite are trying to create human robots who act out of a manufactured response to think they are thinking for themselves.

Joseph C. Sharp is a scientist that volunteered for tests and experiments involving mind control. They were carried out at the Walter Reid Army Institute of Research. Dr. Sharp stated that he could hear and undertook commands sent to him in an echo free isolation chamber via pulse electromagnetic waves sent directly to his brain. Technology like this can be used to make groups of people start killing each other.

South Side Chicago is a perfect example. It has earned the name "Chiraq" because of the war-like shootings taking place daily. The number of killings are so high that they equate to the number of causalities in wars taking place in the Middle East. There are either assassins in Chicago hunting our young so-called Black males or these youth are being triggered through mind control to kill each other. Those are the only 2 options to explain what is going on in Chicago at the moment.

Allen Dellus was head of the C.I.A from February 26, 1953 to November 29, 1961. He was very obsessed with how to control human behavior and spent most his life figuring out how to apply mind control to the masses. While in office he poured billions of dollars into different projects specializing in brainwashing. By the 1960's, mind control was nowhere near as advanced as the Russians who had the technology to send messages by electromagnetic pulse waves telling a subject who was at a distant location exactly what he had to do. The C.I.A. carries out mind control experiments on involuntary subjects all across the wilderness of North America. After I have named all the forms of mind control and the people subjected to it, if you ask yourself if you fit into any of these categories, the answer will be YES.

Involuntary Subjects
- Children
- Ill-informed Persons
- Prison Inmates
- Service Men

Forms of Mind Control
- Brain Concussions
- Brain Implants
- Deep Sleep Therapy
- Electronic Brain Stimulation
- Electro Convulsive Application
- Electric Shock Treatment
- ELF Radiation
- Hypnosis
- Psycho Surgery
- Radio Frequencies Broadcast
- Sensory Depravation
- Stress

By looking at the list above, it would seem that we all have been affected by mind control. This is exactly the point of this book. Everyone has been brainwashed and conditioned. It's all about what do you do to break the conditioning and change the programming provided by Western civilization. We must get our minds back by handing over the mind the devil gave us and rehabilitate our Original mind. Most victims of mind control go insane.

This explains the high ratio of mentally-ill people in the wilderness of North America. We are literally witnessing a nation-wide mental break down caused by years of mind control and manipulation.

I want to go into more information on a less sinister mind control device that is just as effective as any other technique. It's called Tell-Lie-Vision (Television). The television is generally regarded as harmless by people who are not informed. It is, unfortunately, used as a babysitter for your children.

Dr. Ernest Hilgard is a famous researcher on hypnosis. He once said: "Sitting quietly with no sensory inputs apart from the television screen is capable of getting people to set aside ordinary reality, allowing the substitution of some other reality that the television will offer. Your imagination gets so infested and you lose touch of your surroundings and outside world."

Other experts have proved that the more we are surrounded and bombarded by television ads, the less we notice them and the more we are affected by them. The process begins when these television ads begin to bypass the conscious mind and enter straight into the subconscious part of the mind. This leaves us wide open to government programming by projecting images it deems desirable right into the minds of the masses.

For the most part, when people come out with information regarding brainwashing and mind control, they are met with disbelief. This happens because it's hard to believe that a government that is supposed to work for the people, is really working to destroy the people. It forces you to see the reality that the people that make laws also break them.

An American doctor by the name of Hal C. Becker has proved, in a series of experiments, that it is possible to get information to the brain without the targeted person ever knowing about it.

Inner Directional Conditioning was perfected by the Tavistock Institute for Human Relations along with Long-Range Penetration. With these two methods, it was possible to program an entire nation and turn that nation away from its intended course of action. This technique is used to keep people of African-decent from connecting with who they really are. Overall, this is the main reason why we have the mind of the European.

Chapter 10: The Illusion of Progress

Where are we getting the idea that we are making progress as a people? When you talk about slavery to most people, the common answer is, "that was in the past" or, "times have changed". However, what has really changed since we have been free from physical bondage?

Right now, as we speak, more Original people have been to jail than physical bondage during slavery. That means, in 2014, we have more slaves now than we did during the Trans-Atlantic slave trade. Once you go to jail, you lose all privileges that come with being a citizen of your country.

We are coming to a close for the first volume of this ten book series. I would like to close out with talking about the illusion of inclusion. It seems Original people haven't made much progress in the past years. This is due to the fact that we think we are holding each other back from each other's success. In actuality, we should really be studying the detrimental effect of the white supremacist system.

We as a people really think we have made it. We think we have an equal opportunity when it comes to jobs, education, and better standards of living. We have a so-called Black president who helps the gay community more than he helps the so-called Black community. Obama should be held accountable for not helping to improve the living condition of so-called Black people in the U.S. In fact, every president that has come before him ensured the interests of their race of people (White people) were served. In doing this, they also ensure the power structure always works in their favor. The joke is they don't need to come out and say who they are going to help. Studying their deeds and actions will help one observe that the powers that be are helping their people out as much as possible. At the same time, they turn a blind eye to all the brutality that Original people suffer from on a daily basis.

The problem is we have externalized our power and are looking for an individual to save a whole entire nation (when we know that is impossible). It takes a group of people to break down a system set up by an oppressor or an invader. We must unite and work together in order to win this war. This all starts with winning the war in your mind. It means taking back your Original mind and giving the European back his mind. The advantage that white supremacy has benefited from is the masses falsely hoping that things will change but never do. It has been the same since Western civilization has been the dominant power.

We truly believe that White people have changed over the years. Since the end of slavery, we have failed to realize that these white people we see today are the children of the slave masters. They benefit from what their forefathers left behind. In today's time, White Supremacy is hard to detect because it can come in many shades of skin colour. I am not surprised when I see a so-called Black man defending the evils that the Europeans have done to Original people within his 6000 years of being on planet earth.

This society will pay an educated so-called Black man to tell the masses that we have made progress since slavery and that it's our 'Nigger ways' that are holding us back. The same so-called educated Black intellectual will make you believe you can achieve the same success as Jay-Z and Oprah.

After the civil rights movement, the powers that be decided the best way to give so-called Black people the illusion of progress is to constantly feed us so-called Black celebrities. Bill Cosby, Oprah, and even BET are really funded and controlled by White power. Shows like *Girlfriends* and *The Game* also fall into this category.

They give us extremely rich Black people in the media to make other so-called Black people feel like it's their fault why they haven't made it. Someone defending Jay-Z might say, "he used to be a drug dealer from the Marcy Projects and now he's a multi-millionaire. Therefore, White Supremacy can't be the reason why I'm not a multi-millionaire." The truth is the only time a Black man can be a multi-millionaire is if he is entertaining White people.

If you look back throughout history, every Black multi-millionaire had to follow the rules of Western civilization and "sell out". Now, it seems like selling out your people is the normal thing to do.

Music coming out in these times is becoming more and more negative. No one is holding these artists accountable for the negativity they are spreading amongst the listeners. A man like Rick Ross shouldn't be able to rap about putting drugs in female's drinks and still have a career. That means the millions of people buying his records either support that behavior or they are brainwashed to support that behavior.

Some people claim to only hear the beats and not lyrics. However, studies have proven that music is the only form of energy that can enter your subconscious without your permission. This means you have no choice if you receive the message or not. The subconscious mind picks up everything and internalizes it.

I feel like the music industry is partly to blame for the retardation of our people because a positive message is so hard to find in today's music. Everything about the music business is materialistic and none of it is owned by so-called Black people. It is a bunch of White Jewish men who are behind the scene. They are making a living off of the talent of so-called young Black men who never had much growing up. Most of these artists will leave the music business with no money because they had to spend money keeping up with the image of success.

For instance, just recently, an up and coming artist by the name of Bobby Shmurda, claimed he was performing at shows every day and not getting paid for them. This is happening because his record label is taking all the money from him.

Record labels operate like the bank: they loan you money and you have to pay it back once you start making sales. Also, a rapper by the name Tyga, claims his record label, Young Money Cash Money (YMCM) is holding him hostage. Since the inception of the music industry, our people have always been robbed.

Another aspect that adds to the illusion of inclusion is classism. This term was coined by Karl Marx. Classism is all about ownership, having wealth, and who has more than the other person. When you look around the world, as sad as it is, so-called Black people don't own anything. We do not mass produce anything significant enough to build an economic empire for ourselves.

The stress levels of our people struggling to live up to the standards of Europeans are causing us to have early deaths. Statistics show that White people in the U.S. live longer than so-called Black people.

Black elitism started around the end of slavery. This takes place when a group of free Blacks felt they were better than those who were still enslaved. This developed into what Dr. Umar Johnson calls, "The Black Aristocracy". Aristocracy is a form of government in which power is in the hands of a small, privileged, ruling class. The term derives from the Greek word, "aristokratia", meaning rule of the best. Umar lists five areas of society in which they have the most influence on people. They use the intellectual Black in the area of academia to tell the rest to study in the White education system so they will no longer be viewed as a "Nigger" to the police force. They would tell our so-called young Black males to pull up their pants in order to avoid racial profiling. What we are forgetting is that our ancestors have been tortured and lynched wearing suits. Therefore, what so-called Black people wear doesn't stop them from being targeted, brutalized, and even murdered. In fact, no matter how educated or well-dressed you are in the eyes of Europeans, you will always be considered a "Nigger".

Religion is another arena that is conquered by the so-called Black elite in the wilderness of North America. We're taught that our problems don't come from white supremacy. Our problems come from being a sinner. You are encouraged to repent, worship, and are promised that Jesus will, one day, come down and rescue you from your troubles. Most of these pastors are stealing money you barely have from you while molesting children on the down low and sleeping with other people's wives. "Conspiracy" is the only word that came to mind when I saw that New York has a church, literally, on every street corner. With the amount of praying so-called Black people do to Jesus, you would think God turned his back on us. I always questioned if our people were praying to the same God as the slave master. I question it because I wonder whose prayers are being answered. I mean, if White people are praying to same God as so-called Black people, then it seems God favors Whites over the so-called Blacks.

Another aspect the so-called Black elites hide behind is status and titles. Status and titles make you look like you have more power than you really do. Most so-called Black people were convinced that equality arrived once Obama got elected as president. Many of the same so-called Black people turned their backs on him once they realized he was no different from any other presidents. Presidents aren't made to help so called Black people out or the masses in general. They're here to be the face of a corporation called the United States of America.

The number one rule for so-called rich Black elites is to spend their wealth with Europeans because if they use their wealth to uplift fallen humanity, they will eventually have a hard time making a living.

The last census showed that 317 million people live in the U.S. So-called Black people make up 39 million out of that 317 million. Here's where it gets interesting: there are 35,000 so-called Black millionaires out of the 39 million so-called Black Americans. That's only one tenth of the one percent of the population. I was very disturbed when I saw these statistics because none of the 35,000 so-called Black millionaires built an African based school system or invested their money in some of our rising freedom fighters such as Dr. Umar Johnson and Aseer, The Duke of Tiers.

Out of the 35,000 so-called Black millionaires, one hasn't given back to the so-called Black community because they are either not allowed to or don't care to. Regardless of the reason, these so-called Black elites are being controlled. In fact, these are the same so-called Black elites telling other so-called Black people that it only takes hard work to get to where they are. What they're not telling you is that they sold out for that money. In this society, you can't be a millionaire without serving Western civilization. We need to get it out of our heads that it is possible for us to obtain wealth through hard work. These so-called Black elites are paid by White supremacy to make you fall for this illusion.

It is going to take a nation to change this system through unity and a collective objective in mind. Until we are united on the basis of having a common enemy and wanting the same end results, we will be stuck in the same position for years to come.

The first step in healing is acknowledging the problem. The one common problem we all face is Western civilization and White supremacy. They operate off of people being misinformed and mentally ill. Like never before, we are witnessing mass mental breakdowns in today's world.

My main goal in writing this book was to make you ask yourself questions you already had the answers to. Once you realize you have been programmed to behave and act the way you have been, you can replace that European program with the ancient program of knowledge of Self. We must condition our mind and reverse the brainwashing and programming we have suffered from. It will not be easy to reverse but knowing that you have been programmed is the beginning to an uphill battle. The more information we have, the better decisions we can make in life. Once our mentality is restored back to the glory of our ancestors, we will have what it takes to make sure we don't support this devilish society.

We should get back to only spending your money amongst your people. We should start seeing strangers as brothers and sisters and be willing to help out your people in any way possible. The only way to worship God is to treat your fellow man as if he is God. That is how you build a nation. A nation that has its foundation on the principles of Love, Truth, Peace, Freedom, and Justice, will certainly thrive. The U.S. is only 237 years old and has never known peace since its inception. We, as Original people, have millions of years of history and have had 1000's of years of peace on the planet. We are naturally a people of peace who have always followed the universal principles (such as the law of cause and effect and the law of mentalism).

Once we go back and start following the ways of our ancient forefathers, the world will start healing and a real revolution will occur. Things will not change without a little bit of bloodshed. Salvation starts in the mind. Once we free our minds, our conditions will follow.

Peace.

Tell the Truth, Shame the Devil

The Secret Covenant Letter

"An illusion it will be, so large, so vast, it will escape their perception"

1. Those who will see it will be thought of as insane, We will create separate fronts to prevent them from seeing the connection between us. We will behave as if we are not connected to keep the illusion alive. Our goal will be accomplished one drop at a time so as to never bring suspicion upon our selves. This will also prevent them from seeing the changes as they occur. We will always stand above the relative field of their experience for we know the secrets of the absolute. We will work together always and will remain bound by blood and secrecy. Death will come to he who speaks. We will keep their lifespan short and their minds weak while pretending to do the opposite. We will use our knowledge of science and technology in subtle ways so they will never see what is happening. We will use soft metals, aging accelerators and sedatives in food and water; also in the air. They will be blanketed by poisons everywhere they turn. The soft metals will cause them to lose their minds.

2. We will promise to find a cure from our many fronts, yet we will feed them more poison. The poisons will be absorbed through their skin and mouths; they will destroy their minds and reproductive systems. From all this, their children will be born dead, and we will conceal this information. The poisons will be hidden in everything that surrounds them, in what they drink, eat, breathe and wear. We must be ingenious in dispensing the poisons for they can see far. We will teach them that the poisons are good, with fun images and musical tones. Those they look up to

will help. We will enlist them to push our poisons. They will see our products being used in film and will grow accustomed to them and will never know their true effect. When they give birth we will inject poisons into the blood of their children and convince them it is for their help. We will start early on, when their minds are young, we will target their children with what children love most, sweet things. When their teeth decay we will fill them with metals that will kill their mind and steal their future. When their ability to learn has been affected, we will create medicine that will make them sicker and cause other diseases for whish we will create yet more medicine. We will render them docile and weak before us by our power. They will grow depressed, slow and obese, and when they come to us for help, we will give them more poison. We will focus their attention toward money and material goods so they never connect with their inner self. We will distract them with fornication, external pleasures and games so they may never be one with the oneness of it all. Their minds will belong to us and they will do as we say. If they refuse we shall find ways to implement mind-altering technology into their lives. We will use fear as our weapon. We will establish their governments and establish opposites within. We will own both sides. We will always hide our objective but carry out our plan. They will perform the labour for us and we shall prosper from their toil. Our families will never mix with theirs.

3. Our blood must be pure always, for that is the way. We will make them kill each other when it suits us. We will keep them separated from the oneness by dogma and religion.
We will control all aspects of their lives and tell them what to think and how. We will guide them kindly and gently letting them think they are guiding themselves. We will foment animosity between them through our factions. When a light shall shine among them, we shall extinguish it by ridicule or death, whichever suits us best. We will make

them rip each other's hearts apart and kill their own children. We will accomplish this by using hate as our ally, anger as our friend. The hate will blind them totally, and never shall they see that from their conflicts we emerge as their rulers. They will be busy killing each other. They will bathe in their own blood and kill their neighbors for as long as we see fit. We will benefit greatly from this, for they will not see us, for they cannot see us. We will continue to prosper from their wars and their deaths. We shall repeat this over and over until our ultimate goal is accomplished. We will continue to make them live in anger through images and sounds. We will use all the tools we have to accomplish this. The tools will be provided by their labor.
We will make them hate themselves and their neighbours. We will always hide the divine truth from them; that we are all one. This they must never know! They must never know that color is an illusion. They must always think they are not equal. Drop by drop, drop by drop we will advance our goal. We will take over their land, resources and wealth to exercise total control over them. We will deceive them into accepting laws that will steal the little freedom they have. We will establish a money system that will imprison them forever, keeping them and their children in debt. When they shall ban together, we shall accuse them of crimes and present a different story to the world for we shall own all the media. We will use our media to control the flow of information and their sentiment in our favour. When they shall rise up against us we will crush them like insects, for they are less than that. They will be helpless to do anything for they will have no weapons.

4. We will recruit some of their own to carry out our plans. We will promise them eternal life, but eternal life they will never have for they are not of us. The recruits will be called "initiates" and will be indoctrinated to believe false rites of passage to higher realms. Members of these groups will think they are one with us never knowing the truth. They

must never learn this truth for they will turn against us. For their work they will be rewarded with earthly things and great titles, but never will they become immortal and join us. Never will they receive the light and travel the stars. They will never reach the higher realms, for the killing of their own kind will prevent passage to the realm of enlightenment. This they will never know. The truth will be hidden in their face, so close they will not be able to focus on it until it is too late. Oh yes, so grand the illusion of freedom will be, that they will never know they are our slaves. When all is in place, the reality we have created for them will own them. This reality will be their prison. They will live in self-delusion. When our goal is accomplished a new era of domination will begin. Their minds will be bound by their beliefs, the beliefs we have established from time immemorial. But if they ever find out they are our equal, we shall perish then.

THIS THEY MUST NEVER KNOW. If they ever find out that together they can vanquish us, they will take action. They must never, ever, find out what we have done, for if they do, we shall have no place to run, for it will be easy to see who we are once the veil has fallen. Our actions will have revealed who we are and they will hunt us down and no person shall give us shelter. This is the secret covenant by which we shall live the rest of our present and future lives, for this reality will transcend many generations and life spans. This covenant is sealed by blood, our blood. We, the ones who from heaven to Earth came. This covenant must NEVER, EVER be known to exist.5 It must NEVER, EVER be written or spoken of for if it is, the consciousness it will spawn will release the fury of the PRIME CREATOR upon us and we shall be cast to the depths from whence we came and remain there until the end time of infinity itself.

Made in the USA
Middletown, DE
12 January 2024

47322246R00066